Sonder
A Collection of Poems

By

Catherine Keller

NFB
Buffalo, NY

ISBN: 978-0-9996208-9-2

Sonder/Keller-1st ed.

1. Poems. 2. Poetry. 3. Verse.
4. Keller 5. Female Perspective

NFB Publishing/Amelia Press
<<<>>>
119 Dorchester Road
Buffalo, New York 14213
For more information please visit
nfbpublishing.com

Sonder

the realization that each random individual is living a life as vivid
and complex as your own.

TRIGGER WARNING

This book is dedicated to anyone who has had to fight any kind of mental illness. Elements of this book may have triggers for people with histories of self-harm, rape, bullying, drug abuse, eating disorders, and other mental health problems. If you feel like you are still distressed by an experience similar to what you read here, please tell someone who can help you. Please proceed with caution.

Please keep an open mind while evaluating other controversial topics on social injustices such as sexism, homophobia, capitalistic corruption, poverty, segregation, and various sociologically and economically proven inequalities.

The Poems

Vexes

We're always chasing, killing and craving time
There will always be bullies
Whether it be in the sandbox
Or the Senate.

No one dies on time
It's either too early
Or too late.
Hell is crowded
Heaven is scarce
The poor deserve to be rich
And the rich deserve to be poor.

Chocolate and wine make life
A little more bearable
But of course
Those raise your cholesterol
But it's the price to pay
For a sliver of happiness.

We destroy our surroundings and each other
Our trees, our animals
To build cities and corporations
Demolishing green to make green
Exterminating other species
To satisfy our selfish desires
Melting our wildlife, north and south
Flooding our carelessness.

Continuing to fix our flesh
With an aroma of ignorance in the air
With luscious lies and terrible truths
On the radio and TV.
Veterans come back with emotional scars
And nauseating nightmares
Victims are penalized
When it should be the predators.

We are all competing for jobs
With whoever has the most
Expensive piece of paper
And days consist of
Coffee stains and mindless driving
Numbers do not define who we are
Our GPA, income, weight
But that is not us!
We should not be scared to have opinions
And no is a word that's heard too often
And not spoken enough
And we are harsh, because the world is back to us.

Pen to Paper

Isn't ironic?
Writing about writing.
We are all someone else's
Entertainment.

As much as I crave praise
I can't handle it
Because I don't believe the words myself.
Some say writing under the influence
Is cheating
And maybe it is
Maybe I have no real talent
I guess I'll never know.

I put a little bit of myself
In each of my characters
Does that make me conceited
Or lack creativity?
I wish I could write about
Exotic royalty
Edgy motorcycle gangs
Roaring twenties mafias
Psychics and hippies
And Native American tribes
But I'm not creative
Or knowledgeable enough
To do or say what I want.

I will never measure up
To Fitzgerald, Gillian Flynn or Vonnegut
But I'm damn sure
Going to try.
I am destined to go
From riches to rags
The American nightmare.
But I will not let my dream
Go to the cemetery of passions past.

Artists who can no longer create
Are dead because their voice
Has been revoked.

Ghost

People are not homes
They cannot always keep you
Out of the cold
Because sometimes they are the reason
You can't stop shivering.

You can't hurt me,
My soul is made of steel
Do your worst to me
It has taken years for me to feel
Better.

You slithered inside my head
And trickled into my dreams
You are the ghost in my cigarette smoke
That slipped through my mouth
Now I can only manage to dream
Of places to catch my breath
And refresh my troubled mind
But for now I will stain my teeth
With cheap red wine.

Wondering why you plucked me off the shelf
And never bothered to look passed my bruised binding
And the only thing he'll take away from this
Is how I take my coffee and how I hold my pen.

Girl of Your Nightmares

You don't want me
And I don't deserve you
Because I will break your heart.

I don't mean to, but I will
I am a cliché girl
With an appetite for affection
But I frequently squander it with starvation
I will wrap myself in your hoodies
I will steal sips from every drink
I will make you shower me with kisses
I will share my fries with you
I will watch your favorite movies,
And convince you to watch mine.

I will raid your playlists
And show you my own
I will make tea for you in the morning
I will show you my favorite cafes
I will crack jokes with your friends
I will play paintball and laser tag with you
I will play with your pets
I will watch you play guitar
And take pictures of you when you're not looking.

But I am not your dream girl
I will disagree with you
I will not tell you how I really feel
Until I have had too much to drink
I will push you away and run back to myself
When my emotions become too much to bare
I will cry far too often
And make you cry alongside me.
I will smoke and drink too much, even though you despise it
I will complain about my body
I will become wildly furious
I may scratch or bite you too hard
I will not show you most of what I have written
I will not let you control me.

I will not belong to you
I will hang out with my guy friends
I will have coffee breath from time to time
I will wear things you don't like
I will forget to shave my legs
I will laugh too loudly
And I will break your heart.
I am the girl of your nightmares.

High School Sour Hearts

One never made time for me
Another never wanted to leave my side
A few just wanted a body to bang
Another just wanted a chance to hold my hand.

One left me for the class slut
Another left me for a girl who had sex in a Porta-Potty
And three of them played guitar
And me.
One hated rock music so that didn't last very long
Two guys tried to cheat on their girlfriends with me
And three crawled back.

One organized his shoe collection
But hardly had his own life together
And said I love you after three weeks
And on the fourth week
He called me a drunk, depressed little girl.
I have bad luck with Italian guys
And even worse luck with boys
Who thought they were men
And they would rather call me 'baby'
Than by my name.

These are my high school sour hearts
Whom I dated out of boredom
Not infatuation
Because I thought that was what I was supposed to do
And at the time, I didn't respect myself
Or them.

I never had a date to a dance
Or a kiss under fireworks
I never got a romantic mixtape
All I got were a list of blocked phone numbers
And closet kisses.
I needed them to harden my heart
Because it was much too soft
And it's a wonder why
I don't trust anyone.

Attachment

Is the cheap fluorescent streetlight
that illuminated the parking lot
And her glassy eyes which reminds him how
she locks her eyes on something insignificant to
keep her from crying and how she hated being called baby
because she was proud of her name
but she reminisces his embrace as she
squeezes his hoodie and tries not to
glance at her phone to look for his name
while he choked on words that scorched his throat
like when she walked in on him curled up on the
tiled bathroom floor and how he
looked up at her and said he missed her because this winter
has been hard on both of them which tickled his gag reflex and he
felt fire in his esophagus like the flame
he used to spark the problems
he would stuff in his pipe just to forget and when people ask him
how he's doing he responds and says he's fine he's always fine
because there's too much going on to pay attention to and
we're all plagued by problems we weren't prepared for.

Cold

His once bright blue eyes
Fought the gray that clouded them
Depersonalized and desensitized
He had the face of a boy
Who was forced to be a man too soon.

The taste of Camels and Black Velvet on his tongue
The tattoo of Raoul Duke on his forearm
As a reminder not to fear or loathe
The crucifix around his neck
His beautifully raspy, menthol melody of a voice.

He showed me the tattoo on his chest
Of the word 'family' in Chinese
Then told me how he hardly had one
Held at gunpoint at seven years old
With his father's finger on the trigger
On the streets at sixteen
And how hours earlier we snuck into a church at one in the
morning
The open door to a needed safe haven.

Defeated and dopamine depleted
Recovery and relapse
An on and off again relationship
With his beloved heroine
A serotonin incinerator.
Grandma's trying to kill the wrong kind of pain
Forcing them both into early graves
With Munchausen by proxy and a half pack of smokes.

When he returned with no opium and scarce opportunities
He cut his hair and shipped himself off
Distracting with a self-enforced draft
Just as he started smiling again.
I thought my lips were his momentary fixation
Narcotic and nostalgic
But he was a gem, not a junkie
Blistered by heartbreak.

He was probably born
With goosebumps on his bones
And all I could remember
Was how I held him as he shivered.

Muses

I have kept many men warm
Between my thighs
You may criticize
My dopamine distribution
Their doses of happiness
They escape into me
How I listened and soothed them
How I cared for them
How I revived them.

Writing letters to one in rehab
Cleaning him up
Becoming his new heroin
When he was still with her
He was silent and ashamed
The letter he wrote to me unleashed waterfalls
Like the ones we were supposed to see together.

An abstract artist who amused me
When I took care of him when he was coming down from a trip
And he cried into my lap that he missed me
He was rich with desolation
And gave me everything
But what I needed.
I crushed him more and more into the powder-filled capsules
That dominated his empty stomach
And morph him into an insensitive succubus
That fed off my body and starved my soul.

Once he discovered the one in the wings
The one who satisfied my appetite for affection
Who adored me and would move the moon for me
Just so I could see it better.
He was a saint who ignored my sins
Who secluded me from the others I needed

Love is a luxury
That I can never acquire
I don't have the time nor the energy
To torment myself at the expensive of hormones.
They will always be the first
To put their hand on my thigh
And remember the color of my eyes.
The joke is on me because the whole time
I just had to love myself.
But who says female writers can't have muses?

Spite

I will scorch you dry
I am a vixen with a vengeance
Who comes as rare as her steak
Smokey eyes that could smolder you whole.
I'm attracted to places I'm not supposed to go
I build the bridges I need
And burn the ones I don't.

I'm a pacifist in the mosh pit
But I will not hesitate to break you
Like you tried to.
My name means 'pure'
But I am anything but.
Yet somehow even the finest liquor can't help you forget my name.

I was the manic pixie dream girl you couldn't pin down
Your repulsive flatulence is enough to make me
Swipe your credit card and buy twenty pairs of combat boots
That I can wear when I kick down your door
And snatch your mason jars and your blue capsules
After I combine your shampoo with Nair
I wish you nothing but shattered pipes, dry markers
Flat tires and carpal tunnel and you will
Never be able to touch a goddess ever again.

The next one you force-feed out of your grimy hand
Will have bumps on her forehead that are bigger than
The ones on her chest and crooked teeth that bite too hard
Who can ride a horse but not a man
As spiteful as I may be
It is excruciating to remain resilient
And I now understand why some people become recluses
I can see why some people take vows of silence
And give up on talking
To anyone
At all.

Clean

An empty fridge, an empty stomach
Overprotected and oblivious
To what's outside the chipped front door.

Scissors, lighters, and empty bottles
Cluttered under the bed
The scale is a monster
Reading lies
Spelled out loud and clear
Evicting what remains into the porcelain throne.

It's a miracle at all how you're alive
After mopping up the blood that stained the tile floor pink
And how we managed to get it out of the carpet
In the house that was never quite home.
In and out of twelve step
Clean and pure as snow
An unpolluted mindset
Refusing to stoop so low.

You ejected all the poison
That was coursing through your veins
From your scissors, cries and tear streaked eyes.
Within this, one can see
How dark the mind can truly be.

Cardboard Coffin

Sometimes I wonder if anyone will show up
I don't want to play melancholic melodies
I would rather have Blink182 over the stereos
And I want orchids, not lilies.

I imagine only ten people at most will come
But I'm all right with that
No one should make a fiasco out of my disappearance.
I want cross eyed pictures of me propped up
Not the ones of me smiling
I want to be wearing sweatpants in my cardboard coffin
Not my best little black dress.

After the wake, I want to be cremated
And have my ashes spread along a waterfall
So my soul can pass on to its next adventure
Preferably in a more egalitarian universe.
I want everything I have ever owned to either be donated
Or be auctioned off to my friends and family
And I will allow my organs to be donated
To be used for the magnificence of science.

I promise that when I die
I won't be letting anyone down
And I want no tears to be shed
They should be celebrating my release.

Empty

It's getting harder to get through each day without crying
It takes too much energy to even talk and no one really seems to
get that or care
I'm just so tired all the time but I have trouble sleeping through
the night.

I feel my talent slipping away
I keep thinking about crushing up my meds and snorting them
To see if that will make a difference
I think about texting old friends just to talk
But I feel like I have nothing to say.
I'm getting tired of fighting the same battles
And sometimes I feel like all I have left are my razors and my
wrists.

Dragging my ass day by day
Forcing empty enthusiasm and pathetic small talk.
My nerves are numb and my eyes are empty
And the subtle hum of self-hatred
Is sneaking back in.
My brain is bloated by thoughts I want to banish
I'm teetering on the edge of insanity.
Failing to control the voice in my head
That has a hard time talking.

My own tears tease me
Releasing rusted memories
Of moments that I drink to forget.
I've been drowning in martinis and my mind for so long
I have forgotten how to swim,
Who I am loathes who I have been
Do not judge me because I sin
Differently than you.

Sleeping is my séance
And despite the constant quiet
It is the only time I am at peace.
I am living a pathetic excuse for a life
Where the highlight of my day is going to bed.

Hollow

Sometimes, I wish I was made of clay
It would make it easier to slice off unwanted skin
I could shave off the bumps on my nose
And shed a few inches off my thighs
Painlessly and perfect
But that's how it starts.

The mirror mocks my efforts
For trying to stay thin
Taunting reflections filled with lies
Optical illusions that never leave your mind
Cracking the mental calculator that determines
How much nutrition I earned that day
Pretending I'm not punishing myself
For not being petite enough.

Thinking you don't deserve dinner
Like food isn't fuel that helps you function.
But if I just had one bite—
Stop, don't touch that
Nobody loves a girl who's fat.
Not every calorie counts
If you cough it up in time
And feel guilty for questioning the sugar
In the Tic Tac you popped in your mouth right after
Regurgitating desserts I had to learn not to regret.

I feel my fullest when I am hollow
When my stomach growls at my lack of self-respect
And my supper soaked in stomach acid
But I tried my best to be quiet
I didn't even have to wipe the floor this time.
Comparison kills what little self-esteem clings on
Reminding me that my metabolism can never catch up
To my own criticism
And how I liked that cigarettes made my stomach flatter
So someone would want to see me naked someday
And eventually I found her in the mirror.

But food is not the enemy
Beauty is not confined to Photoshopped celebrities and flawless flesh
Your body is magnificent
Be grateful for this machine you have been blessed with
Count your limbs and fingers
Our skin is not meant to constrict us
Sacrificing your body to the cosmetic gods is not the solution
So love the body that is trying to love you back.

Stalling

Hiding in bathroom stalls
Has become a habit for me
The cold tiled floor
And the shrieking of the stall door closing.
Silently praying that no one comes in
So you can have some time to yourself
Even if it does smell like too much bleach
And misaimed urine
Flashing back to eating my paper bag lunch
Because I couldn't find anyone to sit with.

Those close four sides
Are awful for anxiety attacks
Claustrophobia gets the worst of you.
My only companions are the burned-out bugs
In the cheap ceiling lights
The loud silence
And the soap dispenser that never completely
Washes the blood off of your hands.
Don't stare at yourself in the mirror for too long
The lighting doesn't flatter you.

When the bell rings and kids pour through doors
The background hum of pointless conversations
Scares me to death
Because I don't know which one of them
Is next to come in.
In between and during classes
I'll be there
Hiding from the sounds of clacking high heels
And responsibilities.

Listening to people cackling in the halls
Wondering why you couldn't be a part of it
Girls come in giggling about last weekend
And you wish you knew what was so funny
The ultimate exclusion
You on one side of the stall
Them on the other side, clueless as to who you are
Or if you're even there.

Seasonally Defective

Her eyelashes litter the bathroom sink
Her pinkies are dirty and she has holes in the seams of her pants
Specs of blood on the backs of her shirts and brittle hair
This entire year has been an out-of-body experience
Plagued by a blank brain
She can only write when the sun makes an appearance
She withers in the winter
Dissociated and deficient
Meandering with a murky mind
Slushy sidewalks and pale, faceless people
Here in this hypothermic hell.

She doesn't want to pay someone to tell her
What she already knows
Exercise, get enough sleep, take vitamin D, improve your diet
Have you had any suicidal thoughts
Or thoughts of wanting to harm yourself?
"Of course, I'm just tired and uninspired," she wished she could say
Trapped in a town with little to do and too many rainy days
And excessive roadkill
Where people are proud of their prejudice.
She had chameleon eyes that hid behind suburban suicide
Nights of serenades from the downstairs silver
When her skin itches the most
Careful not to get the blood on the sheets.

She smoked in her Subaru one clear night
And saw a shimmer dance across the dark clouds
And she wished for happiness
Then realized
Talking to shooting stars doesn't make things happen.

Have No Fear

Without fear, we could have anything
Do anything, and be anyone
Anyone but who we are
Because fear is what's stopping us.
Set fire to your fears
For you are the smoke who sets sail for the sky.

People can be afraid of chins, knees and venereal disease
And the fear of long words happens to be thirty-seven letters.
You can be petrified of opening your eyes
Even if it meant you never get to see a sunset.
You can be fearful of being afraid
Because what's not to be afraid of?
People can be scared of money
Because money can morph the world into monsters
There are those afraid of clocks
And I can see why since we're always racing it
Some can fear opinions
Which is understandable in a close-minded society
One can be frightened by looking up
Because we have no idea what really goes beyond the clouds.

People can be terrified of loneliness
Because sometimes all we're left with is ourselves
Some of us are afraid of ugliness
Because in some cultures, beauty equals fulfillment
You can be afraid sleeping
Because who knows if and when you will ever wake up?
Those who are petrified of church
Feeling as though they are part of a crowded cult
People can be scared of freedom
Because that word has not been defined quite yet
Some of us are frightened by teenagers
Because one day, they will be in charge.

There are those terrified of knowledge and ideas
Either because the ideas may fail or they may be mocked for having them
There are people afraid of gaining weight
And the number eight, or even being a size eight.
Fear is the flesh-eating virus of life
It feeds off of you until you're too petrified
To step outside of your front porch
It consumes you until you crumble
But my knees will not buckle.

I am not afraid of spiders or clowns
I am not afraid of guns or ghosts
I am not afraid of you or your fists
I am not afraid of you or your words
I am not afraid of the dark or loneliness
I am not afraid of never finding love
I am not afraid of monsters under my bed
Because one sleeps on top of it
I am not afraid of drugs or bad neighborhoods
I am not afraid of war or the apocalypse
I am not afraid of public speaking or the president
I am not afraid of Bigfoot or aliens.
There are over 540 fears
And yet the only thing I'm afraid of is myself.

Reminiscence

I have a horrendous memory
They say depression deteriorates the temporal lobe
But I distinctly remember
The salty taste of the flesh on my fingers
Coaxing the half-digested Doritos
Up my throat and into the trash.

I remember slicing my skin with silver
That promised a release so sweet
My mouth started watering
I remember thinking
This is what I deserve.
I remember the taste of my first cigarette
And that it wasn't to fit in or look cool
I figured I would be dead in a year anyways
So one wouldn't hurt.
I remember looking down at my chest
And wondering when my femininity would sprout
When the girls around me were blooming
I remember saying no to that guy at that party
Who clearly did not understand the meaning of the word.

I remember being slammed up against a locker
In the girls room after gym during middle school
And no one bothered to help me
I remember choking down that first pill
Thinking 'this is what I have to do now'.
I remember having all thirty-seven pills in my sweaty palm
Thinking that this should be enough
I remember waking up and being covered in red splotches
From where I tried to rip my skin off the night before
Thinking that would liberate me.

I remember all of the gin that I drank
To try to prevent me from remembering
I remember not caring, then caring too much
I remember being in my psychiatrist's office when she asked
"Have you had any thoughts of suicide or wanting to harm yourself?"
And the measly 'no' that slipped passed my lips
When I hacked myself two nights prior.

I remember thinking it had to get better, right?
Thankfully, I don't remember all of it
The nights that were hard to forget
And although I slip up on birthdays and names and appointments
I never forgot my serotonin solution
Because I never forgot that I wanted to recover.

Picture

The walls in my parents' house
Are adorned with my communion pictures
Grinning and nine years old
It's hard to believe I managed to get any bigger.
A picture says a thousand words
But can a photograph tell a lie?

I think to myself when I see old photos of me
Keep smiling, kid
You won't be for much longer.
I care so much for those around me
Maybe to make up for lost time
I spent not caring at all.
It's funny how I tell people to be happy
When I can't even take my own advice
I would sell my soul so I could pay my rent.
What I would give to not care at all.

I spend a lot of my time
Trying to make others laugh
Because it's hard for me sometimes
To even crack a smile
There is just so much pain
That screams to be noticed
I feel like the only one paying attention
To the faces of silent shrieks
Knowing I am as powerless as they are.

Blocked

The creative well is all dried out
Hiding the truth in plain sight
Seasons change and so do we
In this dysfunctional paradise.
Another day about to be wasted
As a fading youth
Trapped within these ink-splattered pages.

Broadcasting thoughts that cannot find the right words
Paid opinions of tomorrow
Attempts at a perspective
That everyone will agree on.
Sailing through to Saturday
On caffeine and heavy eyelids
And a mattress that keeps serenading me
Believing my talent is like an empty pen
All dried up.

Scribbling incoherent sentences
Surfing through in silence
The blank page taunting me
The blinking cursor mocking me
My laptop screen numbing my eyes.
Working with words I need to wander for
A flurry of frustration furrowing my brow
Paychecks only flow when the words do
And sometimes writing feels like I'm trying
To staple water to a tree.
For now, I am stuck staring at the ceiling fan
Like it has the answers I'm looking for.

Don't Ask, Don't Tell

When they ask you why you're sick
What it feels like
Tell them you have a parasite lurking in your brain
That feeds off of negativity
That makes mirrors come with labels
That say 'images are larger than they appear'
That forces your fingers down your throat
That begs you to slice your skin like piece of meat
On a plate that you refuse to touch
Like your blood is venom that just won't drain.

It is constant exhaustion
Meaty talons coiled around my neck
A soul trapped in a corpse
Tell them it's claustrophobia of the universe
Simultaneously shrunken and spacious
That it is a constant pity party
That it feels like something swirling in your blood
And decaying in your brain
That it feels like there is sewage in your system.

Tell them it is a mattress that serenades you
Persuading you to be unproductive
That your skin feels like saran-wrap when you're sober
Your throat closes up like it is being squeezed
Like the noose you tried to fit around your neck
But when you are intoxicated
You can finally shed your shell
And be free from yourself
From the flesh that fits like it is four sizes too small.

Tell them it feels like
You have been injected with indecisiveness
The twisted paradox
Of being told to die
And begging to let me live.

Here's Your Sign

You didn't want them to find you
With bullet holes or a wringed neck
Less of a mess to clean up
Less of the hassle you thought you were
And when the doctors slice you open
And find intestines filled with pills
Mouths will drop and tears will spill.

Your parents will keep your bedroom door shut
Because they will get nauseous just from walking passed it
It will take months before they are ready
To pack your clothes in cardboard boxes.
They will have to clean out your locker
And throw out the birthday present
They never got the chance to give you.

Your house will be a shrine
Quick glances at your pictures on the wall
Your mom will be beside herself
Thinking she could have done something more
Your friends won't talk to anyone for weeks
Your brother and sister wouldn't dare venture into your room
Just like you told them to do
It will be as if yellow caution tape
Is wrapped around everything
That reminded them of you
With too many 'sorry for your losses'.

Your parents will never get to hug you when you graduate
Congratulate you on your wedding day
Or hold your firstborn child
You will never see who you wanted to be.
Your favorite songs and movies will be strictly avoided
Because the memories of you will be too fresh
No matter how much time has passed.

You said to yourself
'At least they won't have to pay for my college
Just my coffin'.
No grandparent should have to be
At their grandchild's wake
Praying for revival.
You will be dressed up in your favorite sweater
And they will put concealer on you
As if it would make up for the fact
That the color has long drained from your face.
People you thought who hated you
Will be at your funeral sobbing
Do not wait until you are dead
To realize you are loved.
You were looking for a sign, weren't you?
This is it.

Do not let this disease devour you
Do not let the cackles control you
Do not let your worst nights keep you
From seeing the best days of your life.
Do not let the bullies beat you down.
On days you doubt your strength
Remember how many days
You were forced to hold your own head up
And how far you have made it.

Every day you wake up
Is a nightmare defeated
Continue to defeat.
You are not merely an expense
You are not worthless
You are beautiful
And your life matters.

Strong

A collection of nick knacks
Doesn't make a place home.

No one should be fearful to go home
Home is supposed to be a sanctuary
With laughter and love served for supper
Not a place that dishes out
Bruised knees and sore cheeks.
'I fell' and 'I'm fine'
Becomes words with an all too familiar taste
As it drifts off of the tongue
Rough day at the playground
And come home for round two.

Shoved into a closet
Pulling clumps of hair from your scalp
Screeching words puncturing your eardrums like daggers
Tossing me around like a corpse I'll be one day.

If you can get through this day
You can conquer tomorrow
After being told that you better find
A rich man to marry someday
Because you're useless and hopeless
And I know there's people out there
Who have it much worse
Hiding bruises and reopened wounds
Bringing them to show and not tell
And they can do it because 'they said so'
And that we should respect our elders
But they should be happy that we're fortunate enough
To have more than they did growing up
Jealousy should not be an issue
And they say we cannot get mad
But how can we smile when our teeth are falling out?

We're not allowed to be upset
We're not allowed to be anything else but us
We can only speak when spoken to
Otherwise, we should be stoic, flesh wearing robots
Battered and boneless.
There's a line between discipline and abuse
There's a difference between punishment and throwing punches
Other kids go through it, too
Coming to school all black and blue.

But you will not be pushed down
You are not worthless or weak
You will stand up and fight back
Because that's who you are; strong.

Trenches

No matter how many vegetables you eat
No matter how many flights of stairs you climb
It might be waiting for you at the top
To knock you back down
Walking for a cause and charity cases
Ribbons and bald heads.

Life is not beautiful
Because death is a part of it
The people who least deserve it
Fight the most
When people like me get off easy
When I should be the one
In the hospital bed.
I sound selfish, making it about me
But all I want is to take their pain
And make it my own
Because I'm wasting away as it is
And I'm used to handling pain
And they have so much ahead of them
But they should be making wedding plans
Not writing their wills.

I have utmost respect for warriors
Who are in the trenches with a terminal illness
And the last thing we need
Is to go to another funeral.
But you get in that ring
And put on your gloves
And punch the poison out of you
Until you are left standing.

Gray

I have never seen so much misery in one room
And it smells like piss and rotting memories.
Hoarse throats wailing
'I want to go home'
Constantly forgetting
That this is where they live now.

Wandering around slowly in a wheelchair
In this withered skin
With these shrunken people
Some don't even know their own name.
This is no home
This is gray mashed potatoes for supper
The 'Price Is Right' reruns
And assistance going to the bathroom
Bingo is the highlight of their week
And if their children remember to visit
Or care to.

But who would want to come here?
Even the residents want to leave
But they are so confused
They can't find their glasses.
No one makes friends here
Because they don't know who is next
To fall into that coveted eternal coma.

Life after Eviction

Empty houses
Empty souls
Crowded sidewalks
Of spikes and bones
Not a penny thrown
Not a nickel dropped
Only cracked smiles of the garbage pickers
From cheap vodka that deludes
The taste of poverty.

Condensing your belongings
To a single cardboard box.
People have no sympathy for bums
They always assume
That they're drunks or junkies.
They never think
That maybe life did them wrong.

They say to get a job
But no company would hire someone
Who doesn't own a suit or shower.
And maybe they become a junkie or drunk
Because it helps dissolve the disappointment
That they have become.

Elizabeth

I once knew a girl who wouldn't talk
Not because she couldn't
But because she learned every time she would
No one would listen.

She had sapphire eyes
That spoke volumes
She was too smart for the delinquents
Asking why she wouldn't talk.
After a while, it wasn't because they didn't care
It was because she didn't.
She smoked Newports
And wore a smirk that could make you tremble.
She learned to make them fear her
Like how they used make her fearful.
She filled her body with toxicity
Because she forgot what it felt like to live
And she wanted no part of it.

She wore plenty of black
Her mind was colored grey
Red tissues littered the floor
And for the longest time
That was the only color in her life.
But how could I know her
If she refused to speak?
Her silence said enough.

The Girl I Knew but Never Got to Know

Hair color different every month
Faded slits on her wrists
Thin as a twig, but packed away ice cream
Like she was born to do it.
A boyfriend who wasn't good enough
Habits that were bad enough
To grab my attention.

It frustrated me how shy she was
Because all I wanted to do was talk to her
The music that buzzed through her wires
Was a merely a prologue to her story.

An effortless artist
Forced into something else
But being a hopeless romantic
Does that to a person.
She long boarded
And stole a six pack from some guy
Who deserved it.
She had a brother in jail
A pretty purple bowl
And snuck out regularly
She must have learned from the worst.

She was so incredibly beautiful,
To the point where I couldn't decide
If I wanted to be with her
Or be her
It's a shame she likes guys
But maybe that's another secret she's hiding.

Earbuds

There was a girl in my graduating class named Jean
In Scottish, her name means a gift from God
And she was, but she was often used for target practice
For spitballs, crayons, and pencils.
Her house was chipped and eroded
And kids often ding dong ditched it.

She was in my sixth-grade class
I never gave her my number
Because it was my first year having friends
And I didn't want to lose them
By associating with someone who didn't have any.
She was called a teachers' pet
Because they were the only ones who would talk to her
And on the last day of sixth grade
The teacher hugged her as she cried quietly
And said, "You can do this".

Two years later, the friends I had were gone
Because I couldn't keep up with their cruelty
And she was in my eighth-grade science class.
People snickered when her panties were exposed when she sat down
And she stopped raising her hand in class
To draw less attention to herself.
One day, Jean asked me how I was
And we talked for a bit
And she said she wished she could be pretty like me
But I had frizzy hair, acne and braces
And I told her that she was beautiful
And how this world is cruel
Kids and teachers alike chewed us up and spit us out
But we both knew beauty equated to power
And we were weak warriors.

There was an entitled girl who lived near me
Who relished in wrecking self-esteems
She would mock other girls in the halls and on the bus
And sent them notes online telling them
That they deserve to die
I was bombarded with them
And I'm sure Jean was another victim
But I want Jean to know that karma got her so good.

She had a girlfriend during freshmen year
And people made gagging noises when they kissed in the halls
I'm happy Jean had lots of partners who thought she was beautiful
Because they saw her soul, not the size of her jeans.
We didn't cross paths again until senior year in the bathroom
I was smoking in a stall and she was on the phone
Sobbing and begging the person on the other line to pick her up.
Jean dropped out before she could toss her hat in the air
With the rest of us
And I'm glad she wasn't there.
She was better than us.

There was an eccentric little girl who was adorned in cheetah print
And sparkles who wore green and blue hair extensions to school
And sometimes she talked a little too loud
Because she was used to people not listening to her.

She believed a chunk of her brain was missing
That kept her from solving problems.
She got accustomed to talking to walls
And she'd like to think they listened
Because no one else seemed to.
They made fun of her height, stutter, clothes and blue hair
She was told to straighten out her crooked face
And she would stare at herself in the wretched mirror

Hoping that one day it would.
Now she has a parasite eating at her self-esteem
Telling her she'll never be good enough
And after countless evaluations
They prescribed her a swallowed solution
For her slacking serotonin levels
But didn't give her earbuds so she could ignore the screaming lies.

To eradicate the thoughts with therapeutic frequencies
Because music can teach you to love yourself again.
She knew there were too many victims
Of self-mutilation
And when I had enough
I crowned myself vigilante
Of all those ever mistreated
And did unto others as they have done to us
Revenge has always been my favorite dish.

Some of us made it to graduation
Some of us thought we would be six feet under by now
And the ones who needed muzzles
Should not be the reason we could not make it.
We are the voices people chose to ignore
We are the ones who deserve more than participation awards
We are the ones who soaked our pillows every night
We are the ones who don't want to live in the skin we're in
We are the ones who will no longer be silenced.
Stick and stones may break my bones
But words are the bullets that can shatter your sanity.

Mother Nature

Blue hair and Goodwill sweaters
She loved her candles and incense
And walked barefoot whenever she could.
She brought her pipe everywhere she went
And people came to her
So she could design their tattoo ideas
I have never seen someone draw quite like her.

She preferred Marlboros
And taught me how to meditate
And her mom struggled on food stamps.
She loved to sing underrated indie songs
And her liver was a black hole
Jager was no match to the abyss in her stomach
That she often filled with coffee and Lucky Charms.
She slept maybe three hours a night at best
And her hands never quit shaking
She taught me more about Buddhism
Than any other book I read on it
We called her Mother Nature
And it fit her like her thick sweaters
And I remember when I told her
How I had never felt like I had a family
She held out her arms
And said "welcome home".

She never came across someone she did not try to care for
And as much as it helped them, it hurt her
And their agony made her tremble
And how vodka wasn't enough to fill the void
For the girl who cared for everyone else
She could not care less about herself
And I hope one day she takes that train ride
She always wanted to go on
So she could get away from them
And herself.

Canal

The sky and the water met
To reflect each other,
With shades of periwinkle and faded orange
Along with an old sky watching
A motionless ceiling of the world.
I watched it on a Sharpie-d wooden dock
Of names added together
And doodles of yin yang signs.

One day I pulled the cap off of a marker
And attempted to draw my sun and moon signature.
It's my not-so-secret hide out
Perfect for meditating, smoking, writing, and escaping
The occasional orchid is littered among the weeds
And you'd see empty Labatt cans adorning the rocks
If you went on the right day.
One day I was there and three guys on kayaks with boxed wine
Came up to me and pulled out a ukulele
And started serenading me.

It's my test to see if someone is worth my time
When I bring them to the canal
And if they stare at the rippling water
I keep them
If they are glued to their phone
I never see them again.

Another day, I scratched something off my bucket list.
I got a piece of paper and wrote a message on it
And tucked it in an empty Marley's Mellow Mood bottle
And tossed it into the canal
And watched it slowly bob down.
I won't tell you what I wrote
But the person who finds it one day can show you.

Grade School Lies

They said if a boy pushes you
That means he likes you
But if he loved you, he would know
He shouldn't hurt the ones he loves.
They said all you have to do is work hard and you will succeed
But what if you work hard then get laid off
Because employees get cut like they are on a soccer team
While others get paid to breathe.

They said pink is for girls and blue is for boys
But what if the gender roles we have been assigned
Do not fit into the mold of who we are?
They said do not talk to strangers
But we were all strangers once.
They said that high school will be the best time of your life
But then why are suicide rates the highest during those four years?

They said that Thanksgiving was a time of being grateful
But surely the natives were not when they were being
Consistently raped, slaughtered and infected by the white mans' ways.
They talk about cannabis like it's crack
But neglect to mention how it can be used shrink tumors and treat chronic
pain.
They said that we were only children
When we are eighteen and supposed to decide
Who we want to be for the next sixty years
And still needed permission to take a piss.

They said you can be anything you want
But you can't be gay, transgender, an atheist, or an immigrant.
They said if you do not perform well in school, then you are unintelligent
But standardized tests only measure three out of the nine intelligences.
They said we should never lie
But why do they keep doing it to us?

Dainty

A small girl with a light-hearted laugh
Addicted to runners high and writing
She loved staring at trees and the beauty in nature.
She was my little bookworm
She got a box of two hundred fifty books
For free at a garage sale
She still hasn't read them all
And the shelf they're on is close to collapsing.

She loved coffee and Indian food
And was an adventurous driver
She was spiritual, not religious
With her healing crystals and tarot cards.
When she was finally liberated
From the ignorant fists that forced her down
She cut her hair and dyed it red
Wore leather jackets and black stockings
Got her dainty nose pierced.

She proved she was not her size
And the color and twinkle returned to her eyes.
I remember when we investigated
The old asylum by her school
And tried to go clubbing in the city
And ended up getting lost and ate pancakes instead.
She had bizarre dreams
And proved all the teachers wrong
Who said she wasn't smart enough to go to college.

Her mind had no doors, gates, or windows
I have never met someone so open to everything
Which might be why she never locked anything.
When we were thirteen, we met for the first time
And she knew too many boys who made her feel microscopic

I knew it was hard for her to smile
But whenever she saw me, she did
And I will never forget the day she told me
She had never met someone so happy
Little did she know, I was used to practicing my grins.

She said I inspired her
And convinced her that life was worth living
She looked up to me
And she had no reason to.

Bellies

Brown eyes are not puddles of mud
Thick thighs are not undesirable
Wild, curly hair is not unattractive
Thin arms are not grotesque.
Small breasts do not make you any less sexy
Large butts do not make you any less beautiful
Unwanted birthmarks do not make you any less human
Acne does not make you any less than perfect
Unshaved legs does not make you lazy.

Big noses are nothing to be ashamed of
Bushy eyebrows are nothing to be ashamed of
Natural hair color is nothing to be ashamed of
Your height is nothing to be ashamed of
Your so called 'defects' are nothing to be ashamed of.

Comparisons are cruel
We do not all look like Barbie and Ken
And the movie stars on the big screen
And half of them have been cosmetically tweaked
Because chasing perfection is what society teaches us.
Beauty enhancers play on our insecurities
Stop paying for the supposed self-improvers
And start loving the body you were blessed with.

Freckles are beautiful
Crooked teeth are beautiful
Bellies are beautiful
Pasty and dark skin are beautiful
And do not let anyone
Tell you that you are not.

Filthy Hands

Her dress did not provoke you
Her body did not force you
And it does not matter if she drank too much
And could not muster the word 'no'.
Do not spike her drink
Because you are too ugly to score when she is sober.

Would you still feel the same if it was done to you?
What if it was your sister, or daughter?
Your wife, your mother, or best friend?
Would it still be all right?
Was the little six-year-old in her nightgown
Asking for it
When her uncle slid his grimy fingers where they didn't belong?

And if it happens to a boy
That does not make him a man
Or anything less than human
It does not mean that he was not 'man' enough
To defend himself
It means that we are pro-rape
For allowing it to happen in the first place.
We raise our men to be domineering
And our women to be cautious
Because this kind of behavior is expected
Not prevented.
We have been handing out chastity belts
To the wrong gender
And after all, birth control pills were originally intended
For men
Because it's their responsibility to reproduce.

They have the nerve to blame a low-cut blouse
For what a man did that could have easily been taken care of
With his own two hands
Like an erection is a chronic condition
That needs to be absolved immediately
But I guess you would rather deal with the teeth marks
On your hand from where she bit you after she screamed 'stop'
Instead of blue balls.

If they confess to you, do not run.
This is a time when they need you the most.
You should be grateful they came to you
And not someone who is paid to care.
Don't you dare think of them
As dirty or impure
Before you take a look
At your own filthy hands.

Freckled

Her children will be very lucky.
She wore ugly clothes
Because she felt sorry for them
And she never talked down to us
And treated us as equals.

She was classy, intelligent
And everything I aspired to be.
I could have shuffled for hours through all the books
She kept at the back of the classroom
And she realized how I was quiet in class
But had the most to say.

She was freckled and loved Fitzgerald
And she was hospitalized for starvation
When she was in college.
When she told the psychiatrist
That she wanted to be a teacher
The psychiatrist said
How dare you.

At the end of the school year
I wrote her a note telling her
That she was my favorite teacher
Because she taught me how to fall in love with writing again
When I felt like giving up on it
And myself.

Love

A phobia is an irrational fear
It is not an excuse
To discriminate towards those
Who differentiate from your preferences.
We deserve wedding cakes
Just as much as anyone else
Because you cannot help how you look
Or who you love.

To feel like you do not belong
In your own body
To be ostracized from a society
That preaches to 'be yourself'.
Censoring behaviors
Terrified of being called out
For being too masculine or feminine.
We are not sinners
For falling subject to love
He said to love thy neighbor
And you may throw the first stone
If you have never sinned yourself
And we are all products of sin
And didn't Jesus have two fathers?

They fear us because we are different
We fear them because they are all the same.
Love is not criminal
Love is patient, love is kind
Love is not meant to be confined.
Some of us cannot help
If their parents choose their gender for them
Or if we do not want to have sex at all
We are not bad parents because we will not force
Our children into a lifestyle they do not want.

They think we are the problem
Because we defy procreation
But the procreators are the ones
Who keep giving birth to us.
We are not confused
We are not degenerates
We are stronger than the cruel
For tolerating ridicule.
We are colorful
We are divine
Love will not make us lose our minds.

Unanswered Questions

What is justice to a cop or a criminal?
What is love to a husband or a whore?
What is religion to an atheist or the faithful abandoned?
How do we know God is real, or even male?
What does it mean to be good in a bad world?
What is truth in a universe full of falsities?
How can one chalk up life to a single transcendental truth
When all we can prove is that time and words exist
And that we can think?

The truth is that we are clueless in a world
Where we think we have all the answers.
Civilization started by trying to conquer
Philosophical questions
And it will end in ignorance
The extinction of the American empire.
Humanity will not fail from famine or war
But from a fear of knowledge
Or reluctance to learn.

Some words simply cannot be defined
Nothing is absolute
Things have meaning
Because we assign it to them
Without us, there would be no definition
For anything
We create categories to make sense
Of what is around us
To simplify and break down
But all it has done is generate more complexities
And questions we cannot answer.

Mankind craved knowledge about the infinite
Seduced our souls to meet the stars
Searched for solutions beyond our own sun.
We have progressed backwards
Instead of forward
With our iPhones isolating us
Making it possible for us to be perpetually trapped
In our own small world
Devoid of wisdom and perspective.
We were supposed to progress to be more effective communicators
But we have stunted our own growth
By being left to our own devices.
And now all we are certain of
Is our own skepticism.

Women

Our lives do not revolve around love
Our lives do not revolve around pleasing men
We are not princesses
Pining for our Prince Charming to come rescue us.
Our bra size should not determine
Whether we deserve love or not
We are lipsticked, mascaraed, blood stained
Padded and pressured.

Femininity is expensive
We do not get off easy
With free dinners and drinks
And if you accept
That does not make you owe him anything
We cannot always bust our way through speeding tickets
And if we use a man the way he uses us
We get called sluts, not geniuses.

Other girls are not competition
We should not be turning against each other
To win a man's approval.
Breast feeding in public is taboo
But that's what breasts are for
Not for male amusement.
We are not ornaments
We are not simply maids
We can be heroes, presidents, and governors
But we are intimidating
Because we morph into monsters once a month
Not because we can mutate the system.

We are considered emotional and weak
But we can create other living creatures
And without us, there would be no men
And it's funny how some of them
Do not respect those who created them.
This does not mean we hate men
It just means we have to act like them
So they are forced to take us seriously.

Revolt against the media
Be another crack in the glass ceiling
And be as hideous as you can be
Because nothing is more unattractive
Than intellect
Because they tell us we are merely breasts with no brains.
Make them fear you
Be the opposite of what society wants
Because nothing scares them more
Than originality.

We were raised to be fighters
In the war on women
This is not a battle against the bearded
It is a struggle against the cynical
Against those who say we cannot.
Do not conform to the criteria
That tell you what a woman is
Eat that cheeseburger
Smoke that cigar
Study chemistry
Become a politician or a plumber
Speak your mind
Cut your hair
Dominate the white house
And redefine what it means
To be a woman.

Race to Equality

You are not made of ivory or mud
You do not need to assimilate
To the institution of hate
'Kill their culture', they cry
To preserve their prejudices
Not for their profound superiority.

Concentrating cultures in time of crisis
Labeling facilities
Where you can wash away your impurities
When their hands were anything but
Isolating those as if they were contagious
When they try to contaminate us
With their criticism.
Bible thumping pilgrims claiming
Jesus will save you
Painting him pale
When he was actually Middle Eastern
But we wouldn't know that
Since Hollywood is whitewashed.

Do not assign negative connotations
To aspects you have no control over.
Embrace our multicultural melting pot
Do not be ashamed of your native language
Do not be ashamed of your traditions
Do not be ashamed of your people
Do not abandon your culture
Because that's exactly what they want you to do.
Do not let the actions of a few,
Define you.

They say to come to America
Home of the free
Free to lynch, victimize and disenfranchise you
And strip you of your identity
And call it justice.
Ignore the bigots imitating our founding fathers
Who discovered discrimination
Not equality.
It's funny how some spend time
Pondering the existence of other beings
On Jupiter and in other galaxies
When certain individuals cannot even put up with the people on
our own planet.

Do not occasionally celebrate
And to tolerate does not vindicate
What has hollowed these grounds.
Pledging allegiance to preconceptions.
Arguing all lives matter
Then blame it on black culture
When it's a culture the white man created.
Redlining isn't just written on maps
It signifies the blood spilled on their streets
Saying their culture is criminal for slinging and selling
But when you're systematically oppressed
Your career paths are slim.

No one is born a savage
No one is born a barbarian
We live in a culture of oppression
Assuming these victims are poor, dangerous
Uneducated, or terrorists.
But they residentially segregate
And widen the gap of wealth where
Being white is essentially a tax deduction
And have the nerve to blame US.
Leave no more crimson on your culture's hands
Riots spark revolutions
But point more fingers.

Bold badges beating down
With their entitlement
Yet we are the ones called 'uncivilized'.
They mock our accents and attire
And imprison immigrants
But they cannot see that without them
There would be no US.
But for all the ethnicities that have been excluded
Racists need not apply.

There are not thirty-six races
Or nineteen or five
There is one
And it is human.

Expensive

Trust fund teens
Who pronounce 'bebe' like bee-bee
Michael Kors bags full of daddy's money
With their low fat, mocha lattes from Starbucks in hand
Avoiding the slush on the sidewalks
To preserve their precious Uggs.

Designed to hate those
Who cannot afford the latest Coach wallet
Clad in Couture, cackling over gossip even more juicy
'What's bigger, her fake boobs or the gap between her teeth?'
Touching up their surface flaws with Sephora palettes
And Victoria's Secret Pure Seduction
Even though everyone knows that their secrets
Involve lots of padding and tissue stuffing.

Tanning booth trips and weekly nail salon appointments
To manicure their majesties
With complimentary critiques
Thinking they are superior to the rest of us
Propped up on their pedestals
Like it was Manifest Destiny.

They treat one hundred dollars like it is pocket change
Expensive labels and paying for Instagram followers
Are what they live for
Bragging about their latest Guess purchases
And their recent trip to the Bahamas
Cringing at the thought of consignment shops
And coupon clipping
Wired to waste what they did not work hard for.
How great it must be
To not feel the need to fight for anything.

They may have more money
But we have motivation.
In a world dominated by dollar bills
All I want is simplicity.

Man Down

Man equals warrior
The word masculine is defined as
Strong, dominant, in control.
It always equates to anger
Fury from being told to 'man up'
Because your version of manly
Was not enough
A life of black eyes and bruised egos.

Meninism is a mockery
Of white, middle class boys
Who police the masculinity of their counterparts
Who do not fight for men of color
Gay and transgender men
Men who are battling mental disorders
Men who have been raped
Men who have been abused
And men forced to be violent and silent.
Instead, they torment feminists on social media
And complain about being friend-zoned.

'Don't be a pussy' they say
Vaginas can push eight-pound objects out of them
By all means, be female genitalia.
'Men don't cry' they say
We have all shed a few tears when we were born
That is more than acceptable
Just because you are not a woman does not mean
You are limited to experiencing a range of emotions.
'Grow a pair' they say
You don't even need one to be considered as a man.
How can you 'be a man'
When your role models are abusive or absent?
How can you possibly 'man up'?

As a woman I can tell you that you are not defined
By how much you bench, what car you drive
How you take your steak or how many women you sleep with.
You are more than your favorite sports team
You are more than the anger in your belly
That society shoved down your throat
By telling you that you are not allowed to feel anything else.
You are more than your height
You are more than your facial hair, no matter how patchy
You are more than your testosterone.
And we wonder why we only shout 'man down'
When one is wounded in war.

Femme Fatalities

I am a woman
Who was taught that I am either a whore or a virgin
I am specified by what is between my thighs
But our society has failed to recognize
That regardless of how many men have been inside
I am priceless.

So I'm a slut for sleeping with two or ten guys?
How dare you criticize
When your condom size
Is an extra small.
Oh, that's a cheap shot?
Go ahead and comment on my bra size
I could not care less.
Insecurity is an unwelcome quest
In my cathedral of a body.
You have no right to define
What is yours and what is mine.

I am a woman
Who was taught to be ashamed of my body count
Because sex equals sin and insecure equals slut
My worth does not depreciate
If a man has to negotiate
His way in.
I am not perched on a shelf
Like my body has never been my own
I am not waiting to be possessed
By someone who does not deserve to caress me.
I will not morph my mold
To fit your criteria
I am not a 'call for a good time'
Because my body's net worth looks like a phone number.
I am not a prude for being selective
Only those who are worthy may pass through my palace gates.

I am a woman
Who was raised in a dress code where turtlenecks
Are appropriate because they are not too tempting
Because men cannot be trusted around bare collarbones.
I am a woman
Who was taught to spend eternity searching for my other half
But all I have to is look down
I was trained to believe my only skills involve
Bleaching, baking and bleeding
And how to dodge the empty beer bottles
That are thrown at me while I'm walking home at night.
They won't shatter me.

I have been brought up in a world
With too many Paris Hiltons
And not enough Queen Latifahs
A world where being Cinderella was more desirable
Than being Mulan
A world that shows commercials of women
Smiling while vacuuming.

I am a woman
After battling my bad hair, braces and small boobs
I learned to be confident but not too confident
Knock me down a peg or two
Because god forbid I love myself
I learned that my body is incredible and an insult
And I start to wonder what the men were taught.
For centuries, my kind has been told
That we belong in the kitchen
That our mouths were not meant for talking
That we are not strong
That we need a man to take care of us
Because we are incapable of doing it ourselves
That we only exist to give birth
That we are alive simply to aid mankind.

We are not entertainment
We are not accessories
We are not our skeletons
We are all shades of beige and brown
We are thin and thick
We are bountiful and beautiful
We are fierce and femme
And when I start to feel hideous
After seeing a Victoria's Secret ad
I think about the old, white men
CEOs of industrial insecurities
Who are profiting from us buying into
The ideology that concealing our predisposed imperfections
Will suddenly make us worth looking at.
So I put down the eyeliner and say
"Let's piss off the patriarchy today".

My Craft

I cannot be confined by church pews
I never felt safe there
I found solace as a pagan
Nature is my sanctuary
My sage, my salt and my spirit.

Our bodies are said to have energies called souls
Energy can neither be created nor destroyed
Our energies are essential to our very beings
Making us pretty damn magical.
Energy transcends time and space
And everything ever created is nature
Nature is energy and energy is magick
So nature is magick
We are nature, we are magick.

Our palms tell us stories of all the lives we have to live
Prayers and spells are on the same platform
They are incantations of intent
Saying five Hail Mary's while counting on a rosary
Is as valid as me making a potion with rosemary
My words carry weight
Every sentence is a spell
I scribble sigils to wish me well
I carry hamsa charms with me wherever I travel
To promote positivity.

The pilgrims escaped to a land proclaiming religious freedom
Only to wring the necks of those who were too free
The media makes a mockery of broomsticks and animal sacrifices
Demonizing voodoo and Santeria
Equating black magick with evil
While pilgrims forced them to convert and assimilate
Christians were killing them.

That is why we are witches
To protect ourselves from persecution
We are the second-class citizens
Who challenge the system that binds us.
I radiate magick
I am connected to the sun and the moon
The tapestry of my life is mine to weave
Witchcraft gives me the tools I need to take control of my life
My soul is celestial
My ancestors protect me
My craft commands respect
And if you think casting spells will send me to hell
Then I will see you there.
Baby, don't make me hex you.

Impoverished

Asbestos infested schools
Curbs cracking from the weight of the poor
Overtaxed and underemployed
Even welfare checks bounce here
Duct-taped cars and broken boulevards
That were once booming
More cardboard signs than street signs
Spikes in corners
And this is supposedly
A great nation.

Faced with foreclosure, famine
And underdeveloped citizens.
This is our beloved toxic wasteland
With vacant streets and 40's in paper bags
Hepatitis inducing tattoo shops
Sullen faces with no more food stamps
Insect-infested couches on the side of the road
Barefoot beggars on the curb
Reeking of cheap cigarettes and charity
And you wonder why they try to cheat the system.

Rusted pipe dreams and scarce resources
Public schools that prep for imprisonment
And their lighter-singed thumbs
Are the only things keeping them warm
In this cold world.
This is the neighborhood where if you see someone running
It isn't to lower their cholesterol.

You say end welfare to starve the lazy
And you have the audacity
To accuse US of poor work ethic
But the thinnest people carry the most weight.
There is no faith here
When the church feeds us lies
Indulgences to excuse our inhumanity
Crowded ERs and police brutality are intertwined
And we wonder why the War on Drugs
Hasn't completely dissolved just yet
Like the chemicals they're crowding their nasal cavities with.

Do thugs have prayers?
Because they certainly aren't heard
Worshipping and devoting only distract
When life becomes a game of credit and debit
And they wonder why we soak our problems
In cheap vodka.

This Is What You Think a Feminist Sounds Like

Real men eat pussy and get paid
We'll stop bitching about rape culture
When you stop being a vulture
Over my body.
There's a special place in hell for fuckboys
The only time men are concerned about rape
Is when their own freedom is threatened
And are petrified of becoming someone else's bitch
If they don't make bail.

Go ahead, make a comment about my tits
You'd be lucky to suck my clit
I'm vulgar, I'm not ladylike
Leave the pantyhose in the past
You're right, a woman's place is in the house
Of representatives
Just to repulse you.

Fuck your dominant male bullshit
Fuck your alpha male archetype
And your hegemonic mask.
I'll singlehandedly castrate your hate
You say you're a nice guy
Five minutes into the conversation so far
And you feel the need to convince yourself
And every other chick at this sleazy bar.

I won't wait until you're in the grave to spit on you
Betray me and there will be a bonfire on your tomb
I will brand you like the girls you called cows
You want to wire our mouths shut unless we're sucking your soul
out
You've declared your war on women with your Machiavellianism,
You say ends justify the means,
To validate your killing sprees.
But we never said we'd fight fair,
How dare you fucking telling us what to wear,
You don't get to mutilate,
Get in line so we can castrate.

Get on my knees and do what?
Honey, I choke on small objects
You think feminists don't get laid
Bitch, we have it made
We got to where we are with little to no aid
I'll light the wick at the end of your dick
You objectify us, we dehumanize you
You are nothing more than the meat you beat
And baby, I'm as tough as a two-dollar steak.

If men are from Mars and women are from Venus
You are not superior because you have a penis.

Tragic Kingdom

Eyes wide shut
While the rich man causes the riot
Crimes of the corporate cult
Of closed eyes and open mouths
That contribute to the chaos.

Living in a jungle of jokers
Angels in ambulances
Artists getting high
Decades down the drain
Swallowed by the clock
While the secrets of the sky
Mock life below.

The American dream varies
Failure to one is success to another
A culture obsessed with collegiate degrees
And politician's playpens with white pillars
Front porch flagpoles that make me question
What you're really fighting for
We are nothing but numbers
Under an illusion of freedom
We are scanned like produce
We are not bar codes
We do not deserve to be labelled.

This is my world as I know it
Justice is on my mind
But my face doesn't show it.

Caged

Their lives incarcerated
Encased in cold metal with scratches on the wall
Burdened inmates
Convicted and confined
Slowly losing their minds
In a temple of suspension
Of trials that time forgot.

Segregation into cells
Apart from civilization
In such a way that it makes rejoining it
Nearly impossible to survive adequately
The war on drugs was never about dope
It's more than cartels and handcuffs
Masses of marginalized men with misdemeanors
Criminalizing cannabis and crippling addictions
Profiting politicians and police officers
A scapegoat to incarcerate
That was meant to rehabilitate
But it only reiterates stereotypes
Of sagging jeans and faded body ink.

Monitoring minorities through racial profiling
Frozen in time
Forced to watch themselves fall behind.
A whole lot of time
For hardly any crime
With three hots and a cot
If you're lucky.
Neglecting those shivering in corners
Revoking rights that were never there
This is the New Jim Crow.

Restricting rebels
The metal detectors are programmed to dismiss
The steel in their chest
The sympathy they lack
While they watched them spread their cheeks
Solitarily confined by
Psychosis and stale cereal
And prevent them from making
Authentic progress.

You are killing men
Their blood seeps through your white pillars
In these concentration camps that are not colorblind.
To isolate will not help them assimilate
Under your Supremacy.

Elitist Lies

You are not free
Liberty lies
We are enslaved by a society
Captivated by capitalism
Funded by a New World Order
Secret leaders slither into society
Keeping citizens in the dark
Afraid to shine light on what illuminates.

Censoring our mainstream media
By injecting fear into the eyes that lie
A world run by sheep
Trying to tame lions
Training us to be cogs in a machine.
Countries run by conmen
Passing bills of bullshit
Herding the sheeple with decoy distractions.
And your prejudicial propaganda
Brainwashing millions into believing
The White lies that wove this House
Pretending to protect the people
When most of these terrorists
Are in fact white
And maybe there was something in the water.

The fathers found nothing
But the declaration of deceit
The injustice system in place is pathetic
A plethora of puppet masters proclaiming 'united' nonsense
The blood of every red herring stained the stripes of a flag
That represents nothing but a false doctrine
With a sadistic staff that is willing to
Compromise its people for profit.
It is not ironic that is illegal to be a Nazi in Germany
But you can be a proud owner of a pointy white hood
In Georgia.

The Constitution was constructed to protect
Those who are better off silent
Those who consistently ostracize, dehumanize, and marginalize
Millions of people
Over trivialities that do not determine superiority.
This document should be considered contraband since
Its very material has been criminalized
A composition that claims liberties must be restricted
In order to remain secure
While the pillars may still be upright
We were never really guaranteed stability.

They are the rebels in our revolution
Who deem anything remotely irreverent as illicit
But when our big brother's fragile ego is wounded
We bleed.

Wake Up & Smell the Corruption

Everything is so divided
Yet it's called "united"
Controlling and manipulative
The hypocrites in Armani
Revolting rhetoric used to get a vote or check
Resisting to transform to what's outside the pillars
Where lions are led by lambs.

These Houses extinguish the fire
Fueled by We the People
With excuses all around
Amendments are irrelevant and democracy's a joke
Constant popularity contests
It's time for a great escape
From these iron webs.
A mongrel nation
No man created equal
Consisting of catastrophes and ill tolerance.

Convince them to crown thy good with brotherhood
Clinging to false security
Amid all failures and unity.
Excessive pride and endless complaints
We live in a Utopia
Where we are Susceptible to corruption
Land of the caged
Home of the cowards.
Morals become meaningless
In an apocalypse through the addiction
Of cash and control
Where money chokes your morals
We are the corporate slaves
Forced into cafes and cubicles
With our nonexistent names.
Scan coded slaves
Who fight to be free.

White Lies

Privilege is when the Latina in Victoria's Secret is closely followed
While I escape with three pairs of panties in my bag.
Privilege is more doors being held open for me by men
When I'm wearing makeup
More comments and whistles when I'm exposing more skin
But somehow that does not feel like privilege
It is more predatorial.

Privilege is speaking vulgarly and not having it attribute
To your education or economic status
It is being able to walk into a salon and not question
Whether someone will be able to cut your hair or not
Or feeling obligated to style your hair in a particular way
So you can be hired.

Privilege is 'cracker' being the worst thing you can be called
It's being able to find liquid cover-up that matches your skin tone
It's not bringing my ethnicity into question if I make a mistake
It's that most of the people in your textbooks looked like just you
It's a direct correlation between the probability
of where you grew up
And the amount of melanin present.

I am seventeen and caught with less than
half a gram of pot on school property
I am assigned five hours of community
service and five days of suspension
While kids with contraband in the
so-called academy get handcuffs.
Privilege is not feeling out of a place in a room full of pale faces
It is how the white man's history is mandatory curriculum
While studying other people's cultures are considered electives
And privilege is how this piece got published.

Why are you complaining about Affirmative Action for why
You didn't get into NYU when really
That order in 1961 was the biggest white lie
James is hired more often than Jamal or Jane.

Privilege is a perk of being pasty
The lighter you are
The less likely you are to be imprisoned
And that explains why jail cells consist of civilians
Who have been marginalized for centuries
For petty reasons.

This is woven into our catastrophic quilt of a country
The assumption of superiority with these carnal corporations.
I've said it before and I'll say it again
We cannot control how we are born
So why are we taxed and mistreated
For not fulfilling our country's criteria?

Hypocrisy

We are the generation obsessed with killing artificial pain
This medicated madness.
We live in a world where people would rather buy Instagram followers
Than a sandwich for a homeless man.
A Siddhartha Gautama tattoo and a Rolex
On the same wrist
We are obsessed with spirit animals
Because being human isn't exotic enough
Buddhist tapestries adorn their walls
But they have never heard of the Four Noble Truths.

We think we know and do not understand
Self-proclaimed wordsmiths
Who need to drink in order to write,
Facebook phonies and Twitter terrorists
The generation of thin skin and thick skulls.
Self-esteems made of glass
People who bleed greed
We waste our time
Trying to find soulmates who don't exist
We are opinionated on subjects we know nothing about
We don't read enough
Constantly complaining
Hoping other people will pick up the slack
Because we lack the motivation to fix
What our forefathers fucked up.

We buy shit we don't need
But neglect to donate
We talk too much and don't speak up enough
We aren't as brave as we think
We lie because we can
And say 'you only live once'
To justify the amount of shots you did
Instead of trying to change the planet you were born on
So you would not feel the need to drink.

Manipulation leads to success
Seldom hard work
We want to travel but we judge other cultures
We want to leave where we are
Because we can't be bothered to solve our own problems
And worst of all
We have become experts on concocting excuses
Not solutions.

Doubtful

Reminiscing of nights with long cars rides
Staring at sparkling streetlights
Listening to old songs
That will never get old.
Thinking about how we were taught to live in fear
And that is why we hardly ever live.

Now I just have nights I won't remember
With people I will never forget.
And I'll be in my room until midnight
Staring at a blank notebook
Waiting for the words to find me.
And all I really want is to go back
To the nights I felt alive.

Nowadays I'm burning brain cells and wasting time
I wake up tired and wired
Pondering how I profit
Off of my framed, pricey piece of paper.
Can I really call myself a writer
For stringing a few sentences together?
Is my true purpose being published
Or picking pennies off the concrete?

I try my damnedest not to let my self-pity swallow me
Secluding me on this island of sedation
Struggling to balance on
The thin line between conformity and madness
In the midst of an identity crisis
The not-so-happy medium
Of psychoanalysis and philosophy
My sense of self disintegrating
Second guessing my passions and my purpose
Those moments my brain feels as though it's boiling
Interferes with my train of thought and veers off
Shacking up with my impulses.

The cursor taunts me when I attempt to type
To say anything of substance
Trying to make my words worth more.

Wander

I wonder what it feels like
To belong somewhere
I was always told that I needed to find my niche
But my nomadic soul
Is doomed to endlessly wander
I was never meant to stay anywhere for very long.

I am adaptable and a loner
And people mistaken me to be devious
And maybe I am
Maybe I deceive myself.
Everyone is segregated into clumps
And I float between them
I don't consider myself religious or a scholar
Wealthy or poor
A junkie or sober
An artist or completely logical
A seductress or a tomboy.

I am a free spirit
I cannot be tied to any label for long
And as much as I want to find other wanderers
We will rarely cross paths
Because we are always moving.
Some call it running away
Going nowhere fast
I call it traveling.
It must be nice to have a home
But my family are the ones who don't quite fit the mold.

Spitfire

The flames in her heart that cannot be contained
That somehow soothes her fiery soul
She is a bubble-popping punk
Her laughter spreads like wildfire
She could singe your psyche
And make you question everything you know
She could spit blood-red venom
With a spirit that could never burn out
Her words would sizzle beneath your scalp
She is a dragon
And you'd be lucky if all she did
Was blow smoke in your face.

She is a pyro punk
And a red rebel
She is a flare gun
Bright and booming
She sparked the Revolutionary cannon
She is the desert and a global warning
Her Fire cracks
And will obliterate its path.
Signaling rebirth with a period of recovery
Singeing the last devious bits.

Do not smother her spirit
For she could scald you on the spot
She is hell in heels
That sprays out of volcanoes
She is wild, untamable, and controlled chaos
She is the serenity in incense and the eternal flame
She cannot be extinguished
And is her greatest weapon and enemy.
It's no wonder they call her
Spitfire.

No

I always envisioned myself being a vanquisher
A soldier of society
Bringing evil to its knees
And justice to its feet
I never wanted to be the damsel in distress
I wanted to be the heroine
Not the helpless.
But 'be quiet' and 'shut up'
Made me believe otherwise.

People have tried to muffle me for too long
Either out of arrogance or fear
But I will not be silenced
I will not be ignored.
I should not be ashamed to be an advocate
I have every right to be passionate
About what I put on paper.
I am a warrior
Who went from stuttering to screaming.

There has always been an internal flame
Fueled by the desire to fight
The others struggle to ignite a single spark
But I can breathe fire.
I used to crave my future coffin,
But now I stay alive just to spite them.

I am a daughter, a friend,
A writer, a girlfriend,
An activist, an independent,
I am a survivor, a fighter
A feminist, a hedonist, a pacifist, and a punk.
I have a voice
I am stubborn
I am beautiful
And I am unstoppable.
My words declare war
My opponents are those who want my mouth sewn shut
Even when my smirk says enough.

And although my job is to play with words
My favorite one is still
No.

Previous Publications

For the manuscript, <u>Sonder</u>

"Pen to Paper"—Teen Ink Magazine, 2015.
"Clean"—Hooligan Magazine, Issue 13, 2016.
"Cardboard Coffin"—The Stray Branch, Issue 19, 2017.
"Stalling"—Slipstream Magazine, Issue 36, 2016.
"Here's Your Sign"—Tipton Poetry Journal, Issue 30, 2016.
"Trenches"—Teen Ink Magazine, 2015.
"Grade School Lies"—Teen Ink Magazine, 2015.
"Filthy Hands"—Red Fez Literary Magazine, Issue 86, 2016.
"Love"—Wilderness House Literary Review, Issue 45, 2016.
"Impoverished"—Pink Girl Ink Press, 2017.
"Hypocrisy"—Pink Girl Ink Press, 2017.
"Doubtful"—Pink Girl Ink Press, 2017.
"No"—Wilderness House Literary Review, Issue 45, 2016.

About the Author

Catherine Keller is 22 years old with a Bachelor's degree in Communications with a minor in Sociology from The College at Brockport. She has had 10 articles published in the NeXt section of the Buffalo News, as well as poetry published in eight literary magazines including *Wilderness House Literary Review, Tipton Poetry Journal, The Stray Branch,* and *Hooligan Magazine.* She was also a social media intern for BP and Esperanza magazines, which focused on bipolar disorder, depression and anxiety disorders. She has been writing creatively for as long as she can remember and is also in the midst of writing ten other stories that will be novels and short story collections (eventually). When she's not writing, she spends her time chasing waterfalls and free food.

Instagram: catiekeller